Mexico

MEGAN KOPP

MEDIA ENHANCED BOOKS

AV2 BY WEIGL

ADDED VALUE • AUDIO VISUAL

www.av2books.com

MEDIA ENHANCED BOOKS
AV²
BY WEIGL™
ADDED VALUE • AUDIO VISUAL

Go to **www.av2books.com**, and enter this book's unique code.

BOOK CODE

S 8 0 9 9 8 0

AV² by Weigl brings you media enhanced books that support active learning.

AV² provides enriched content that supplements and complements this book. Weigl's AV² books strive to create inspired learning and engage young minds in a total learning experience.

Your AV² Media Enhanced books come alive with...

Audio
Listen to sections of the book read aloud.

Key Words
Study vocabulary, and complete a matching word activity.

Video
Watch informative video clips.

Quizzes
Test your knowledge.

Embedded Weblinks
Gain additional information for research.

Slide Show
View images and captions, and prepare a presentation.

Try This!
Complete activities and hands-on experiments.

... and much, much more!

Published by AV² by Weigl
350 5th Avenue, 59th Floor
New York, NY 10118
Websites: www.av2books.com   www.weigl.com

Library of Congress Cataloging-in-Publication Data

Kopp, Megan.
 Mexico / Megan Kopp.
     pages cm. — (Exploring countries)
 Includes index.
 ISBN 978-1-4896-1022-5 (hardcover : alk. paper) — ISBN 978-1-4896-1023-2 (softcover : alk. paper) —
ISBN 978-1-4896-1024-9 (ebk.) — ISBN 978-1-4896-1025-6 (ebk.)
 1. Mexico—Juvenile literature. I. Title.
 F1208.5.K65 2014
 972—dc23
                          2014005944

Printed in the United States of America in North Mankato, Minnesota
1 2 3 4 5 6 7 8 9 0 18 17 16 15 14

042014
WEP150314

Project Coordinator Heather Kissock
Art Director Terry Paulhus

Photo Credits
Every reasonable effort has been made to trace ownership and to obtain permission to reprint copyright material. The publishers would be pleased to have any errors or omissions brought to their attention so that they may be corrected in subsequent printings.

Weigl acknowledges Getty Images as its primary image supplier for this title.

Contents

AV² Book Code 2

Mexico Overview 4

Exploring Mexico 6

Land and Climate 8

Plants and Animals 10

Natural Resources......................... 11

Tourism... 12

Industry 14

Goods and Services...................... 15

Indigenous Peoples....................... 16

The Age of Exploration................. 17

Early Settlers.................................. 18

Population 20

Politics and Government............. 21

Cultural Groups............................ 22

Arts and Entertainment............... 24

Sports 26

Mapping Mexico........................... 28

Quiz Time...................................... 30

Key Words 31

Index 31

Log on to www.av2books.com 32

Mexico Overview

Mexico is a land of extremes, with high mountains, deep canyons, scorching deserts, and lush rain forests. **Indigenous** peoples have lived in Mexico for thousands of years. In the 1500s, Spanish conquerors took control of the land and its resources. Spain ruled Mexico for several hundred years until the people rose up and fought for independence. Today, most people living in Mexico speak Spanish. Some are very wealthy. Others are extremely poor. Located in the continent of North America, Mexico is a country with vast mineral resources and a rich cultural history.

Many of Mexico's best-known dancers and musicians perform at the Palace of Fine Arts in Mexico City.

Mexican painters are known for brightly colored artwork.

The cardón cactus grows in northwestern Mexico. It is the largest type of cactus in the world.

Fruits and vegetables are sold at outdoor markets throughout Mexico.

The scarlet macaw, a type of parrot, is one of more than 1,000 kinds of birds found in Mexico.

Exploring Mexico

Mexico stretches from the Pacific Ocean in the west to the Gulf of Mexico and the Caribbean Sea in the east. It borders the United States to the north and Guatemala and Belize to the south. With a total area of 758,449 square miles (1,964,375 square kilometers), Mexico is the 14th-largest country in the world. The country is wider in the north. The Mexico-U.S. border extends for more than 1,900 miles (3,050 km). The area called the Isthmus of Tehuantepec in southern Mexico is only 135 miles (220 km) wide.

United States

N

Baja Peninsula

Map Legend

Mexico

Land

Water

Baja Peninsula

Sonoran Desert

Copper Canyon

Capital City

SCALE

500 Miles

500 Kilometers

Baja Peninsula

The Baja **Peninsula**, sometimes called Baja California, is 760 miles (1,220 km) long and 25 to 150 miles (40 to 240 km) wide. Mountains extend down the peninsula, and several peaks are more than 9,000 feet (2,700 meters) high. The Gulf of California, also called the Sea of Cortez, separates the peninsula from the mainland.

Sonoran Desert

Copper Canyon

United States

Cuba

Mexico City

Belize

Mexico City

Guatemala

Honduras

Nicaragua

Sonoran Desert

The Sonoran Desert is one of the largest and hottest deserts in North America. With a total area of about 120,000 square miles (311,000 sq. km), it covers a large part of northern Mexico, as well as southern Arizona and California. The desert contains many types of plants and animals that cannot be found anywhere else in the world.

Copper Canyon

Located in northern Mexico, Copper Canyon is up to 4,600 feet (1,400 m) deep. It is larger than the Grand Canyon in the United States. There are few roads in the area, and most visitors see only a small part of Copper Canyon by train.

Mexico City

Mexico City is the country's capital and largest city. More than 20 million people live in and around the city. It is built in a high valley, more than 6,500 feet (2,000 m) above sea level.

LAND AND CLIMATE

Mexico's main mountain range is called the Sierra Madre. It is divided into three smaller ranges. The Sierra Madre Occidental is on the western side of the country. The Sierra Madre Oriental is on the eastern side. The volcano Citlaltépetl, found in the Sierra Madre Oriental, is the highest mountain in the country. A southern mountain range, which borders Guatemala, is called the Sierra Madre del Sur.

A large, dry, flat region in northern and central Mexico is called the Mexican Plateau. Located between the Sierra Madre Occidental and Oriental, the plateau is about 6,000 feet (1,800 m) above sea level. One of the world's most active volcanoes, Popocatépetl, rises from the southern edge of the Mexican Plateau.

The volcano Popocatépetl has erupted more than 30 times since the 1300s.

The Gulf Coastal Plain on the eastern side of the country is a wide **lowland** region with many swampy areas. On the Pacific Coast, lowlands south of the Sonoran Desert make productive farmland. The Yucatán Peninsula in the southeastern part of Mexico is made up of limestone rock that is full of caves and water-filled holes called cenotes.

Due to its size and varied landscape, Mexico has a wide range of climatic conditions. From August to November, hurricanes are common along both the east and the Pacific coasts. Most of the southern half of the country is wet and warm. In this tropical climate, the heaviest rainfall occurs from May to August.

In desert regions in northern Mexico and on the Baja Peninsula, temperatures can reach 110° Fahrenheit (43° Celsius) or more in July and August. The city of Veracruz, on the Gulf of Mexico coast, has an average temperature of 77°F (25°C). Cities and towns in the Mexican Plateau can have average temperatures of about 65°F (19°C). Snow is found year-round on the higher peaks in the Sierra Madre ranges.

The Sierra Madre Oriental range is about 700 miles (1,100 km) long.

Land and Climate BY THE NUMBERS

48 **Miles**
Length of Lake Chapala, the country's largest natural lake. (77 km)

175,000 **Square Miles**
Size of the Chihuahuan Desert, located mostly in northeastern Mexico and extending into southern Texas, New Mexico, and Arizona. (450,000 sq. km)

18,406 **Feet**
Height of Citlaltépetl, which is the third-highest mountain in North America. (5,610 m)

PLANTS AND ANIMALS

E ach **habitat** in Mexico has many types of animals and plants. In the north, the Sonoran and Chihuahuan Deserts have plants such as agave, yucca, and many kinds of cacti. These plants can survive with very little rainfall. Armadillos, deer, mountain lions, coyotes, and many different types of reptiles live in Mexico's deserts.

Large forests of **coniferous** trees grow along the slopes of the Sierra Madre. Tropical rain forests are found in the Yucatán Peninsula and on the Pacific Coast. These forests are home to monkeys, parrots, jaguars, tapirs, anteaters, and other **species**. Many of these animals are declining in number because forests are being cut down for lumber.

Hundreds of species of tropical fish can be found in the Gulf of Mexico off the coast of the Yucatán Peninsula. Other sea animals that live along Mexico's coastline include whales, dolphins, and manatees. Gray whales mate and give birth off the coast of the Baja Peninsula. In the summer, these whales feed in Alaska's coastal waters. The round-trip length of the whales' annual journey is 10,000 miles (16,000 km). It is the longest **migration** of any mammal.

Mexico is home to several endangered animals, including the jaguar. It is estimated that there are only 15,000 jaguars living in nature in the world.

50 Feet

Height of the Baja Peninsula's boojum tree, which is said to look like an upside-down carrot. (15 m)

3,000 Miles

Distance traveled by millions of monarch butterflies each year from Canada and the northern United States to spend the winter in Mexico. (4,825 km)

NATURAL RESOURCES

Materials found in nature that have economic value are called natural resources. Petroleum, or oil, is the most valuable natural resource in Mexico. Most of the country's oil deposits are found around the Gulf of Mexico. Natural gas is also found in petroleum-producing regions.

Mexico's large **deciduous** and coniferous forests are a source of lumber. Trees cut down by loggers include pine, mahogany, oak, and red cedar. More than 9.8 million cubic yards (7.5 million cubic meters) of timber are legally logged each year. Illegal logging, in protected areas where cutting down trees is not permitted, is a serious problem. It destroys more than 60,000 acres (24,000 hectares) of Mexico's forests each year.

Mexico is a leading producer of several minerals. In most years, Mexico produces more silver than any other country. Gold, lead, copper, and zinc are also mined.

Almost **3 Million**
Number of barrels of crude oil produced in Mexico each day. (477 million liters)

160 Million
Number of troy ounces of silver produced each year for use in jewelry, electronics, medical supplies, and batteries. (4,975 million grams)

Mexico's oil wells, on land and in the Gulf of Mexico, account for almost one-fifth of all the oil produced in North America.

TOURISM

Tourism is important to the Mexican **economy**. People travel to Mexico for its culture, beaches, and affordable prices. The country recognizes the value of drawing in tourists. In the late 1960s, the Mexican government began improving **infrastructure** on the Caribbean side of the Yucatán Peninsula. It built roads and an international airport. The government also improved the quality of drinking water and provided waste management services. The first large tourist hotels opened in 1974.

Most of Cancún's resorts are located in the "hotel zone," which extends for 17 miles (27 km) along the coastline.

The area around the city of Cancún quickly became popular with visitors for its warm climate and white sandy beaches. This region now attracts more than 2 million visitors each year. Cancún's success led to additional growth along the coastline. Playa del Carmen, to the south of Cancún, was once a small fishing town. Today, it is filled with resorts and tourist attractions.

The island of Cozumel, just offshore, is one of the world's most popular destinations for scuba divers. Many tourists also visit Chichen Itza and other historic sites in the Yucatán Peninsula that were centers of the ancient Maya civilization.

Most of Mexico's visitors come from the United States and Canada. Popular tourist destinations include cities north of Mexico City, such as Guanajuato and San Miguel de Allende. Visitors to these cities can view some of the country's oldest buildings and learn about Mexican history. On the Pacific coast, the resort towns of Puerto Vallarta and Cabo San Lucas draw visitors searching for a beach getaway. Whale watching and sea kayaking are popular activities off the coast of the Baja Peninsula. Each year, more than 6 million people visit Mexico on cruise ships.

Mexico's first national park, Desierto de los Leones, or Desert of the Lions, was created near Mexico City in 1917. President Lázaro Cárdenas del Río established 40 national parks during the 1930s. Today, hundreds of thousands of tourists a year visit the national parks around Mexico City.

A wide variety of marine life, including sea turtles, can be seen in the Caribbean Sea off the coast of Cozumel.

INDUSTRY

The petroleum industry is Mexico's largest. Much of the oil not needed for use in Mexico is sold to the United States. Since 1938, Mexico's oil industry has been controlled by a government-owned company, Pemex. This company explores and drills for oil. It also runs refineries that turn petroleum into products people and businesses use, such as gasoline.

In recent years, Mexico's oil production has been falling. Pemex has not been able to spend large amounts of money to search for new oil deposits. At the end of 2013, the Mexican government changed its laws to allow foreign companies to explore and drill for oil in Mexico.

Mexico manufactures and **exports** a wide variety of products. These include chemicals, electronics, clothing, and steel. In recent years, Mexico's automobile industry has grown quickly. The country is now the world's fourth-largest exporter of cars.

Many Mexicans work in the agriculture industry. Most of Mexico's land is too dry or rocky for farming, but some crops grow well on the land that is suitable. Sugarcane is grown in many areas of Mexico, and the country is one of the leading sugar producers in the world. Other important crops include corn, wheat, beans, oranges, cacao beans, and coffee. Coffee is Mexico's most valuable export crop. Mexico is also one of the world's leading producers of vanilla. Melons, tomatoes, lettuce, and other fruits and vegetables are also grown.

Industry BY THE NUMBERS

3rd Mexico's rank in 2012 among the largest oil exporters to the United States, after Canada and Saudi Arabia.

5 Pounds Amount of chocolate that can be produced from the beans of one cacao tree. (2.3 kilograms)

3 Million Number of cars produced by Mexico's auto industry each year.

More than 550,000 people are employed by Mexico's automobile industry.

GOODS AND SERVICES

About 80 percent of the products Mexico exports are sent to the United States. In 2012, the value of goods sold to the United States totaled $277 billion. Besides oil, major exports include agricultural products, cars, electronics items, and medical equipment.

Mexico's exports to the United States and Canada have increased a great deal in recent years. In 1994, the three countries signed the North American Free Trade Agreement (NAFTA). This agreement removed many taxes and other limits on trade between Mexico, Canada, and the United States.

More Mexican workers are employed in the country's service industry than any other. Workers in this industry provide a service to people rather than produce goods. Service workers include people who work in stores, restaurants, hotels, banks, schools, and hospitals. Many jobs in this industry are related to providing services for tourists.

Bananas, squash, alfalfa, onions, and many other crops are grown in the state of Morelos, near Mexico City.

INDIGENOUS PEOPLES

NINE
Number of Aztec emperors.

400,000
Population of Tenochtitlán in the early 1500s.

2012
Year the calendar created by Mayan scientists ended.

The first people to live in Mexico were hunter-gatherers. They hunted small game, and they collected wild grasses and the fruit of cacti for food. Over time, people settled in more permanent villages. They began growing corn, avocados, chili peppers, beans, squash, and pumpkins.

The Maya civilization controlled a large area of southern Mexico from about 1000 BC to AD 1500. The Maya developed a system of **hieroglyphic** writing. They also created calendars and made advances in mathematics. The Maya built towns and cities in the Yucatán Peninsula and other areas. Temples for religious ceremonies were often built at the top of large pyramids. Some of these pyramids can still be seen today. After several centuries, the Maya civilization began to decline. Historians are not sure why this happened.

By the 1300s, many parts of Mexico were ruled by the Aztecs. These indigenous people of central Mexico conquered other groups and created a large empire. In 1325, the Aztecs began the city of Tenochtitlán. It was built on an island in Lake Texcoco. The Aztecs made **dikes** to hold back water and filled in marshes to create more land.

Tenochtitlán became the Aztec capital. From this city, Aztec emperors ruled more than 6 million people spread out over 80,000 square miles (207,000 sq. km).

Many structures built by the Maya can still be seen in southern Mexico.

THE AGE OF EXPLORATION

By the 1500s, Spain had established **colonies** on several islands in the Caribbean. In 1518, the Spanish governor of Cuba began hearing stories of great wealth in Mexico. He chose soldier and explorer Hernán Cortés to lead an **expedition** to Mexico to investigate these stories.

Cortés reached Mexico in 1519. At first, the Aztecs welcomed him and his men in Tenochtitlán. Some historians think the Aztecs believed Cortés was a god. In 1520, however, Cortés took Emperor Montezuma II prisoner, and the emperor was killed. The Aztecs then forced Cortés and his men to flee Tenochtitlán.

3 MILLION
Number of Aztec people who died of smallpox after the arrival of Cortés and his men.

3 Months

Amount of time it took Cortés to win control of Tenochtitlán in his final battle with the Aztecs in 1521.

500
Number of soldiers Cortés had when he took over Tenochtitlán.

Cortés returned the next year and took control of the Aztec capital on August 13, 1521. Many Aztec people were killed or taken as slaves. Others died from diseases carried by the Spanish, such as smallpox. By 1525, Spain ruled almost all of Mexico.

Some Spanish adventurers who came to Mexico wanted to find new lands with more wealth to offer. Explorers and then settlers traveling north from Mexico claimed for Spain large areas that are now part of the United States. These areas included California, Arizona, New Mexico, and Texas.

The first meeting between Cortés and Montezuma II has been represented in many works of art.

EARLY SETTLERS

Spanish settlers destroyed some Aztec artwork, but many pieces can be viewed today in Mexico's museums.

The Spanish called their Mexican colony New Spain. Where Tenochtitlán had stood, the Spanish built Mexico City as their capital. Spanish settlers brought new animals, such as horses, cattle, sheep, and pigs. They also brought with them a new religion.

Most people in Spain followed the Roman Catholic faith. Beginning in the 1500s, many Catholic priests traveled from Spain to Mexico to teach indigenous peoples this religion and Spanish ways of life. Throughout northern Mexico, Spanish priests established missions, or settlements, where indigenous people lived and worked.

Missions included schools where children learned to read and write in Spanish. Adults were trained in Spanish farming methods. They also learned trades such as carpentry.

The missions promoted the Roman Catholic religion, but many native beliefs and practices remained. Some ancient religious customs mixed with Christian holidays. All Souls' Day on November 2nd was close to the Aztecs' autumn rituals in honor of departed **ancestors**. From these two traditions came the Day of the Dead festivities still celebrated in Mexico today.

Many Mexicans decorate the graves of family members on the Day of the Dead.

The Spanish government gave large grants, or gifts, of land in Mexico to soldiers, explorers, and other settlers. These huge estates were known as *encomiendas*. The Spanish landlords were allowed to take any profits they could from their estates, including the unpaid labor of the indigenous people who worked in the fields or mines. In theory, the estate owners were responsible for the well being of the people who worked for them. With few exceptions, however, indigenous people were overworked and not well cared for.

In the mid-16th century, deposits of silver were discovered in central Mexico. The city of Zacatecas was started in 1546 after silver was found in the area. Other new settlements followed later discoveries.

Mexico City continued to grow. Some small houses were replaced with mansions for settlers who had become wealthy. The outsides of these homes were decorated with tile, bronze, and colorful stone. Simple churches were rebuilt as elaborate cathedrals.

Only people born in Spain were allowed to hold high-ranking official positions. Even though they were a small minority of the population, Europeans controlled most of the political power in Mexico. Spanish settlers controlled almost all of the wealth as well.

Early Settlers BY THE NUMBERS

About 30,000
Population of Mexico City in 1525.

20% Amount of silver, known as the Royal Fifth, that mine owners in Mexico paid as a tax to the Spanish government.

80
Number of missions in New Spain by 1559.

More than 100,000 people live in Zacatecas today. A church built in the 1700s is one of the largest buildings in the center of the city.

POPULATION

More than 116 million people live in Mexico. This makes Mexico the 11ᵗʰ most populated country in the world. It is the largest Spanish-speaking country. Mexico's population has grown a great deal since 1900. At that time, 13 million people lived in Mexico. However, in recent decades the rate of population increase has slowed. One reason for this is lower birth rates. In 1960, a Mexican woman had, on average, more than 7 children. Fifty years later, the number was 2.4.

Another reason that Mexico's population has been growing more slowly is **emigration**. In the 1990s and early 2000s, millions of people left Mexico to live in the United States. Most emigrants were seeking greater opportunities to find work and earn money. Mexican emigration has declined in recent years because fewer jobs are available in the United States.

4.5 MILLION Population of Guadalajara, Mexico's second-largest city.

93% Percentage of Mexico's population who speak Spanish as their first language.

About 12 Million
Number of people born in Mexico who are living in the United States.

| Traffic jams are common in the densely populated center of Mexico City.

POLITICS AND GOVERNMENT

Mexico became an independent country in 1821, after 11 years of war to end Spanish rule. The new country was much larger than present-day Mexico. However, 15 years later, Texas rebelled against Mexican rule and won its independence. It later joined the United States. From 1846 to 1848, Mexico and the United States fought against each other in the Mexican-American War. Under the Treaty of Guadalupe Hidalgo ending the war, California, most of Arizona and New Mexico, and other areas in the West became part of the United States.

For much of the late 1800s, Mexico's citizens suffered under harsh rulers. They had little freedom, and many people lived in poverty. In 1910, a revolt began against a **dictator** named Porfirio Díaz Mori. The Mexican Revolution went on for years, and different leaders held power until a new **constitution** went into effect in 1917. Nearly one million Mexicans died in the conflict.

Today, Mexico's federal, or national, government is made up of executive, legislative, and judicial branches. The president, who is elected every six years, heads the executive branch. The legislative branch, which passes new laws, includes two houses of Congress. The Senate has 128 members, and the Chamber of Deputies has 500. The Supreme Court of Justice is the country's highest court.

$15 Million Amount the United States paid to Mexico for the land Mexico gave up in the Treaty of Guadalupe Hidalgo.

1947 Year women were given the right to vote in all parts of Mexico.

31 Number of states, plus a federal district that includes Mexico City, in Mexico.

U.S. President Barack Obama met with Mexico's President Enrique Peña Nieto during a visit to Mexico City in 2013.

CULTURAL GROUPS

Mayan dance groups perform traditional dances in brightly colored dresses.

During the time that Spain ruled Mexico, people's **social status** was based on race. The top level of society belonged to people born in Spain. They were called *peninsulares* because they came from the Iberian Peninsula. This is the part of Europe that includes the countries of Spain and Portugal. Next came the *criollos*, people born in Mexico who had Spanish parents or ancestors. At the lowest levels of society were *mestizos* and indigenous peoples. *Mestizos* had mixed Spanish and indigenous ancestry. The *mestizos* and indigenous peoples were often poor, and they did not have opportunities to become educated.

Today, Mexico's population includes many different cultural groups. Indigenous peoples make up 30 percent of the population. Mexicans of European heritage make up 9 percent. About three-fifths of people in Mexico have mixed heritage.

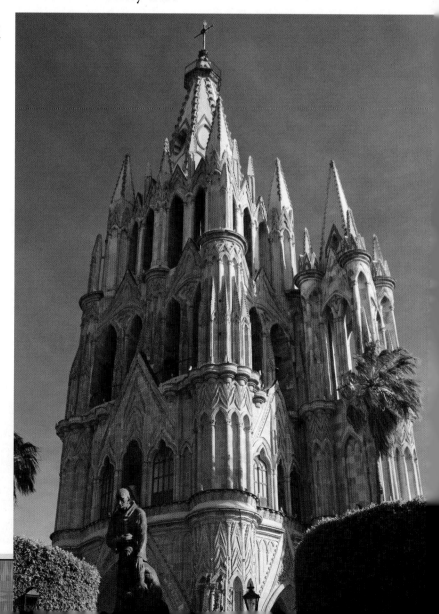

Catholic churches, such as Guanajuato's San Miguel de Allende, are found in cities and towns in all parts of Mexico.

Some of Mexico's indigenous peoples remain isolated from the rest of the country, often due to the challenges of the areas in which they live. Along the coast of the Gulf of Mexico, indigenous groups can be found in the mountains north of Veracruz. Mayan people make up most of the population in some **rural** areas of the Yucatán Peninsula and the state of Chiapas, which borders Guatemala. In rural areas of the Oaxaca Valley in southern Mexico, many villages contain mostly Zapotec people. Most villagers are extremely poor.

More than three-fourths of Mexicans are Roman Catholics, and religious holidays are an important part of the country's cultural life. The two weeks around Easter are filled with celebrations and rituals. On December 12th, Mexican Catholics honor their **patron saint**, Our Lady of Guadalupe. The Feast of Our Lady of Guadalupe features a traditional meal that includes **tamales**, black beans, and a hot tea made with cinnamon sticks and fruit.

Mexicans of all faiths celebrate Independence Day on September 16th. Another national holiday is Cinco de Mayo, which means May 5th in Spanish. It marks the date in 1862 when Mexican forces won a victory over a French army that had invaded the country.

More Than 60
Number of indigenous languages spoken in Mexico, in addition to Spanish.

1% Portion of the Mexican population that is of Asian or African heritage.

About 800,000
Number of Zapotec people living in the state of Oaxaca.

During Cinco de Mayo celebrations, performers may re-create the 1862 battle between Mexican and French soldiers.

ARTS AND ENTERTAINMENT

Mexican artists and writers are known around the world. Octavio Paz was an essay writer and poet whose work focused on cultural issues. Paz was the first Mexican writer to win the Nobel Prize in Literature. Author Carlos Fuentes, born in Panama, became known for his plays, short stories, and novels. His book *The Old Gringo* was made into a movie starring Gregory Peck, Jane Fonda, and Jimmy Smits.

Demián Bichir has been acting since he was 3 years old.

Mexican actors and filmmakers have received international recognition. In 1952, Anthony Quinn became the first Mexican actor to win an Academy Award, or Oscar. Quinn won a second Oscar five years later. One of today's best-known actresses, Salma Hayek, was born and raised in the state of Veracruz. Demián Bichir, who began his acting career at the Palace of Fine Arts in Mexico City, now stars in the television show *The Bridge*. Filmmaker Guillermo del Toro has received numerous awards for his movies, which include *Pan's Labyrinth* and *Pacific Rim*.

The birthplace of artist Frida Kahlo, in Mexico City, has been turned into a museum.

Mexico is also known for its music, from the traditional **mariachi** to Mexican hip-hop and salsa. Luis Miguel is one of the country's most successful singers. He has won five Grammy Awards and four Latin Grammys for his work. Singer Ariadna Thalía Sodi Miranda, known as Thalía, has sold more than 40 million recordings around the world and is one of the best-selling Latin musicians of all time. Thalía is also a successful **telenovela** actress.

One of the most widely recognized Mexican art forms is the mural. These large paintings on walls are often influenced by the art and architecture of Mexico's indigenous peoples. Well-known muralists include Diego Rivera, José Clement Orozco, and David Alfaro Siqueiros. Their works tell the story of the Mexican Revolution, the struggles of the poor, and the country's modernization. Diego Rivera was married to Frida Kahlo, a painter best known for her colorful self-portraits. In 2002, Salma Hayek played the role of Kahlo in the film *Frida*.

Arts and Entertainment BY THE NUMBERS

1947 Year the Mexican Academy of Film gave its first awards for outstanding work in movies, providing winners with a statue called the Ariel.

1990 Year Octavio Paz won the Nobel Prize in Literature.

Thalía received a star on the Hollywood Walk of Fame in Los Angeles, California, in 2013.

SPORTS

Sports have been played in Mexico since at least the times of the Maya and Aztec civilizations. In one Mayan ball game, players had to put a rubber ball through a stone hoop on the side of a court. Losers lost their heads. Today's athletes do not face these kinds of risks, but sports are still taken very seriously in Mexico.

María Espinoza won an Olympic gold medal in taekwondo in 2008 by beating Nina Solheim of Norway.

Soccer is the country's most popular sport. When Mexico's national team is competing in a World Cup or Olympic match, it seems as if all other activity comes to a standstill as millions watch the game on TV. In 2012, Mexico's men's soccer team won the gold medal at the Summer Olympics, beating Brazil in the final game, 2–1.

Mexico's record of Olympic success began in the 1900 Summer Games, when the men's polo team won a bronze medal. In 1968, Mexico became the first Latin American country to host the Olympics. Mexico City was the site of the Summer Games that year. Diver Joaquín Capilla is the most successful Mexican Olympic athlete, with four medals. He is also the only Mexican athlete to win medals in three consecutive Olympics. María Espinoza and Guillermo Pérez each won a gold medal in taekwondo at the 2008 Summer Games.

The game in which Mexico's men's soccer team won the gold medal in 2012 was the most-watched Olympic event in the country's history.

Mexicans also enjoy playing and watching baseball. Many Mexican players have been successful in Major League Baseball in the United States. Pitcher Fernando Valenzuela of the Los Angeles Dodgers won the Rookie of the Year and Cy Young Awards in 1981. He was the first player to win both awards in the same year. In 2013, successful Mexican pitchers included Marco Estrada of the Milwaukee Brewers, Jorge de la Rosa of the Colorado Rockies, and Jaime Garcia of the St. Louis Cardinals.

Bullfighting has been popular since the Spanish brought the sport to Mexico in the late 1700s. Jaime Bravo was one of the top bullfighters of the 1950s and 1960s. Alejandro Amaya is one of Mexico's current leading **matadors**.

Professional wrestling, called *lucha libre*, is popular in Mexico. Masked competitors add drama to the sport with acrobatic leaps. Wrestlers take on the roles of different characters, who may be good or evil.

Pitcher Jorge de la Rosa, born in the city of Monterrey, won 16 games in the 2013 baseball season.

Sports BY THE NUMBERS

2011 Year that lightweight boxing champion Julio César Chávez was inducted into the International Boxing Hall of Fame.

7 Number of Olympic medals won by Mexican athletes at the 2012 Summer Games.

Mapping Mexico

We use many tools to interpret maps and to understand locations of features such as cities, states, lakes, and rivers. The map below has many tools to help interpret information on the map of Mexico.

Map of Mexico

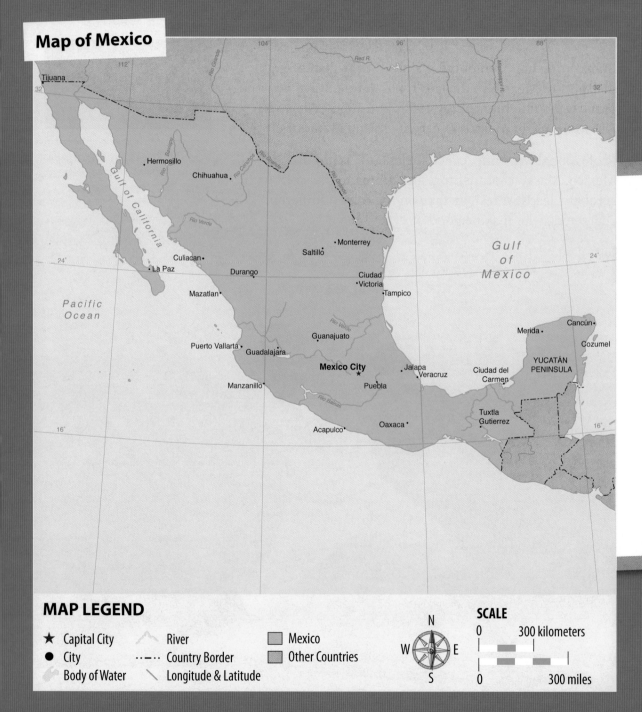

MAP LEGEND

★ Capital City   △ River   ▢ Mexico

● City   -·-·- Country Border   ▢ Other Countries

▱ Body of Water   ╲ Longitude & Latitude

SCALE

0   300 kilometers

0   300 miles

Mapping Tools

- The compass rose shows north, south, east, and west. The points in between represent northeast, northwest, southeast, and southwest.
- The map scale shows that the distances on a map represent much longer distances in real life. If you measure the distance between objects on a map, you can use the map scale to calculate the actual distance in miles or kilometers between those two points.

- The lines of latitude and longitude are long lines that appear on maps. The lines of latitude run east to west and measure how far north or south of the equator a place is located. The lines of longitude run north to south and measure how far east or west of the Prime Meridian a place is located. A location on a map can be found by using two numbers where latitude and longitude meet. This number is called a coordinate and is written using degrees and direction. For example, the Mexico City would be found at 19°N and 99°W on a map.

Map It!

Using the map and the appropriate tools, complete the activities below.

Locating with latitude and longitude

1. Which city is found at 21°N and 87°W?
2. Which island is located at 20°N and 86°W?
3. Which city is found on the map using the coordinates 21°N and 103°W?

Distances between points

4. Using the map scale and a ruler, calculate the approximate distance between Mexico City and the city of Oaxaca.
5. Measuring from north to south, what is the approximate length of southern Mexico's Yucatán Peninsula?
6. Using the map scale and a ruler, find the approximate width of Mexico between Mazatlan and Tampico.

ANSWERS 1. Cancún 2. Cozumel 3. Guadalajara 4. 280 miles (450 km) 5. 250 miles (400 km) 6. 600 miles (1,000 km)

Quiz Time

Test your knowledge of Mexico by answering these questions.

1 What is the length of the Baja Peninsula?

2 How large is Mexico in square miles?

3 What is the highest mountain in Mexico?

4 Which pitcher was the first to win both the Rookie of the Year and Cy Young Awards?

5 What is the population of Mexico?

6 Who was the explorer sent by Cuba's governor to Mexico?

7 What is the most common religion in Mexico?

8 What year did Mexico win independence from Spain?

9 Which Mexican poet won the 1990 Nobel Prize in Literature?

10 Which artist's home was turned into a museum in Mexico City?

ANSWERS
1. 760 miles (1,220 km)
2. 758,449
3. Citlaltépetl
4. Fernando Valenzuela
5. More than 116 million
6. Hernán Cortés
7. Roman Catholicism
8. 1821
9. Octavio Paz
10. Frida Kahlo

Key Words

ancestors: members of a family who lived long ago

colonies: countries or areas ruled by another country

coniferous: evergreen trees and shrubs that have cones

constitution: a country's basic laws, which state the rights of the people and the powers of the government

deciduous: trees that lose their leaves every year in a certain season

dictator: a ruler who has complete control of a country

dikes: walls or mounds of earth built to prevent flooding

economy: all of the goods and services that are produced, bought, and sold in a country or area

emigration: leaving one's native country to live in another country

expedition: a journey by a group of people for a specific purpose

exports: sends products to another country to be sold

habitat: the place where an animal or plant is usually found

hieroglyphic: a system of writing made up of pictures and symbols that stand for words

indigenous: native to a particular area

infrastructure: basic structures and facilities, such as roads, bridges, railroads, and airports, that are needed for a country or area to function well

lowland: an area of land that is at or near sea level

mariachi: a type of lively music often performed by street bands and featuring trumpets and guitars

matadors: people who have the leading role in a bullfight and whose task is to kill the bull

migration: movement from one place to another at different times of year

patron saint: a saint believed to protect a certain area

peninsula: a strip of land surrounded on three sides by water

rural: outside of cities or other built-up areas

social status: a person or group's position in society in relation to others

species: groups of individuals with common characteristics

tamales: cornmeal mixed with ground meat or beans and spices that is wrapped in corn husks and steamed

telenovela: a drama-based television show similar to a soap opera

Index

animals 7, 10, 18
art 5, 17, 18, 24, 25
Aztec 16, 17, 18, 26

Baja Peninsula 6, 9, 10, 13
Bichir, Demián 24

Cancún 12
Caribbean Sea 6, 12, 13, 17
Catholicism 18, 22, 23
Chichen Itza 13
climate 9
Copper Canyon 7
Cortés, Hernán 17
cultural groups 22, 23

deserts 4, 7, 9, 10

economy 11, 12

farming 9, 14, 15, 18

Gulf of Mexico 6, 9, 10, 11, 23

Hayek, Salma 24, 25

indigenous peoples 4, 16, 17, 18, 19, 22, 23, 25
industry 14, 15

Kahlo, Frida 24, 25

languages

Maya 13, 16, 22, 23, 26
Mexican Plateau 8, 9
Mexican Revolution 21, 25
Mexico City 5, 7, 13, 15, 18, 19, 20, 21, 24, 26
mountains 4, 6, 8, 9, 10, 23
music 5, 25

national parks 13

Pacific Ocean 6, 9, 10, 13
Paz, Octavio 24, 25
Pemex 14

petroleum 11, 14
population 16, 17, 19, 20, 22, 23
poverty 4, 21, 22, 23, 25

Rivera, Diego 25

silver 11, 19
sports 26, 27

Tenochtitlán 16, 17, 18
Thalía 25
tourism 12, 13
trees 10, 11, 14

Valenzuela, Fernando 27
Veracruz 9, 23, 24
volcanoes 8

whales 10, 13

Zapotec 23

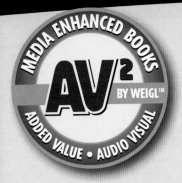

Log on to www.av2books.com

AV² by Weigl brings you media enhanced books that support active learning. Go to www.av2books.com, and enter the special code found on page 2 of this book. You will gain access to enriched and enhanced content that supplements and complements this book. Content includes video, audio, weblinks, quizzes, a slide show, and activities.

AV² Online Navigation

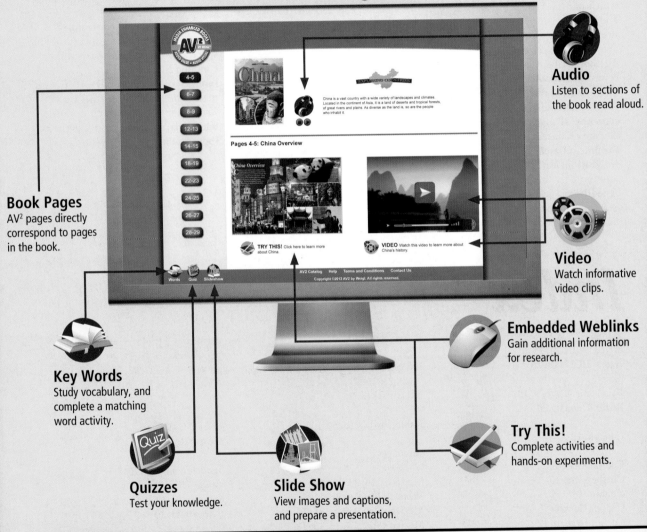

Audio
Listen to sections of the book read aloud.

Book Pages
AV² pages directly correspond to pages in the book.

Video
Watch informative video clips.

Key Words
Study vocabulary, and complete a matching word activity.

Embedded Weblinks
Gain additional information for research.

Quizzes
Test your knowledge.

Slide Show
View images and captions, and prepare a presentation.

Try This!
Complete activities and hands-on experiments.

AV² was built to bridge the gap between print and digital. We encourage you to tell us what you like and what you want to see in the future.

Sign up to be an AV² Ambassador at www.av2books.com/ambassador.